Impressum
Verlag: BABADADA GmbH, Nedderfeld 112 , 22529 Hamburg
Geschäftsführer / Verlagsleitung: Harald Hof
Druck: Books on Demand GmbH, In de Tarpen 42, 22848 Norderstedt

Imprint
Publisher: BABADADA GmbH, Nedderfeld 112 , 22529 Hamburg, Germany
Managing Director / Publishing direction: Harald Hof
Print: Books on Demand GmbH, In de Tarpen 42, 22848 Norderstedt

除
divide

186/2

黑板
board

教室
classroom

校园
school yard

老师
teacher

纸
paper

钢笔
pen

书写
write

办公桌
desk

直尺
ruler

书
book

学生
pupil

书包
satchel

铅笔盒
pencil case

铅笔
pencil

卷笔刀
pencil sharpener

橡皮擦
rubber

画板
drawing pad

图画
drawing

画笔
paintbrush

颜料盒
paint box

剪刀
scissors

胶水
glue

练习册
exercise book

家庭作业
homework

12

数字
number

2+2

加
add

5−2

减
subtract

2×2

乘
multiply

计算
calculate

A

字母
letter

ABCDEFG HIJKLMN OPQRSTU VWXYZ

字母表
alphabet

hello

字
word

课文

text

读

read

粉笔

chalk

上课

lesson

登记

register

考试

examination

证书

certificate

校服

school uniform

教育

education

百科全书

encyclopedia

大学

university

显微镜

microscope

地图

map

废纸筐

waste-paper basket

酒店
hotel

青年旅社
hostel

外币兑换处
currency exchange office

手提箱
suitcase

汽车
car

语言
language

是/否
yes / no

好的
Okay

您好
hello

翻译员
translator

谢谢
Thank you

……多少钱？

how much is…?

我不明白

I don´t get it

问题

problem

晚上好！

Good evening!

早上好！

Good morning!

晚安！

Good night!

再见

goodbye

方向

direction

行李

luggage

包

bag

双肩包

backpack

客人

guest

房间

room

睡袋

sleeping bag

帐篷

tent

旅游信息

tourist information

海滩

beach

信用卡

credit card

早餐

breakfast

午餐

lunch

晚餐

dinner

票

Ticket

电梯

elevator

邮票

stamp

边界

border

海关

customs

大使馆

embassy

签证

visa

护照

passport

飞机
airplane

船
ship

消防车
fire truck

公交车
bus

卡车
truck

汽艇
motorboat

自行车
bike

汽车
car

摆渡船
ferry

小船
boat

摩托车
motorbike

警车
police car

赛车
racing car

租车
rental car

拼车

car sharing

拖车

tow truck

垃圾车

garbage truck

发动机

engine

汽油

fuel

加油站

fuel station

交通标志

traffic sign

交通

traffic

交通堵塞

traffic jam

停车场

parking lot

火车站

train station

轨道

tracks

火车

train

电车

tram

货车

wagon

直升机

helicopter

机场

airport

塔

tower

乘客

passenger

集装箱

container

纸板箱

carton

手推车

cart

篮子

basket

起飞/降落

take off / land

城市

city

村庄

village

市中心

city center

房子

house

电影院
movie theater

广告
advert

路灯
street light

街道
street

出租车
taxi

小吃店
snack shop

行人
pedestrian

人行道
sidewalk

斑马线
zebra crossing

垃圾箱
dumpster

十字路口
crossing

红绿灯
traffic lights

CINEMA

小屋
hut

公寓
apartment

火车站
train station

市政厅
city hall

博物馆
museum

学校
school

大学

university

银行

bank

医院

hospital

酒店

hotel

药房

pharmacy

办公室

office

书店

book shop

商店

shop

花店

flower shop

超市

supermarket

市场

market

百货商店

department store

鱼店

fishmonger's shop

购物中心

mall

海港

harbor

城市 - city

公园

park

长凳

bench

桥

bridge

楼梯

stairs

地铁

subway

隧道

tunnel

公交车站

bus stop

酒吧

bar

餐馆

restaurant

邮筒

postbox

路标

street sign

停车计时器

parking meter

动物园

zoo

游泳馆

swimming pool

清真寺

mosque

农场
farm

污染
pollution

墓地
cemetery

教堂
church

操场
playground

寺庙
temple

地形
landscape

树叶
leaf

指示牌
signpost

路
path

草地
meadow

石头
stone

树
tree

徒步旅行
者
hiker

河
river

草
grass

花
flower

峡谷

valley

山

hill

湖

lake

森林

forest

沙漠

desert

火山

volcano

城堡

castle

彩虹

rainbow

蘑菇

mushroom

棕榈树

palm tree

蚊子

mosquito

苍蝇

fly

蚂蚁

ant

蜜蜂

bee

蜘蛛

spider

甲虫

beetle

青蛙

frog

松鼠

squirrel

刺猬

hedgehog

野兔

hare

猫头鹰

owl

鸟

bird

天鹅

swan

野猪

boar

鹿

deer

麋鹿

moose

水坝

dam

风力发电机

wind turbine

太阳能电池板

solar panel

气候

climate

服务员
► waiter

菜单
► menu

椅子
► chair

汤
soup

披萨饼
pizza ◄

桌布
tablecloth

餐具
cutlery

前菜
starter

主菜
main course

甜点
dessert

饮料
drinks

食物
food

瓶子
bottle

快餐

fast food

街边小吃

street food

茶壶

teapot

糖盒

sugar bowl

一份饭菜

portion

意式咖啡机

espresso machine

高脚椅

high chair

账单

bill

托盘

tray

刀

knife

餐叉

fork

勺子

spoon

茶匙

teaspoon

餐巾

serviette

玻璃杯

glass

碟子

plate

汤盘

soup plate

碟子

saucer

酱

sauce

盐瓶

salt shaker

胡椒磨

pepper mill

醋

vinegar

食用油

oil

调味料

spices

番茄酱

ketchup

芥末

mustard

蛋黄酱

mayonnaise

特价
special offer

顾客
customer

乳制品
dairy products

购物车
shopping cart

水果
fruit

肉铺 butcher's shop	面包房 bakery	称重 weigh
蔬菜 vegetables	肉 meat	冷冻食品 frozen food

冷盘

cold cuts

罐头食品

canned food

洗衣粉

detergent

甜食

candy

日用品

household products

清洁用品

cleaning products

销售员

sales representative

收银机

cash register

收银员

cashier

购物清单

shopping list

开放时间

opening hours

钱包

wallet

信用卡

credit card

袋子

bag

塑料袋

plastic bag

饮料
drinks

水
water

果汁
juice

牛奶
milk

可乐
coke

红酒
wine

啤酒
beer

酒
alcohol

可可
cocoa

茶
tea

咖啡
coffee

意式浓缩咖啡
espresso

卡布奇诺
cappuccino

香蕉

banana

苹果

apple

橙子

orange

西瓜

melon

柠檬

lemon

胡萝卜

carrot

大蒜

garlic

竹子

bamboo

洋葱

onion

蘑菇

mushroom

坚果

nuts

面条

noodles

意大利面条

spaghetti

米饭

rice

沙拉

salad

薯条

fries

炸土豆

fried potatoes

披萨饼

pizza

汉堡包

hamburger

三明治

sandwich

炸猪排

escalope

火腿

ham

萨拉米

salami

香肠

sausage

鸡肉

chicken

烤肉

roast

鱼

fish

燕麦片

porridge oats

穆兹利

muesli

玉米片

cornflakes

面粉

flour

羊角面包

croissant

面包卷

bread roll

面包

bread

烤面包

toast

饼干

cookies

黄油

butter

凝乳

curd

蛋糕

cake

蛋

egg

煎蛋

fried egg

奶酪

cheese

冰激凌

ice cream

糖

sugar

蜂蜜

honey

果酱

jelly

巧克力酱

nougat cream

咖喱饭

curry

农舍
farm house

粮仓
barn

稻草捆
straw bale

田野
field

马
horse

拖车
trailer

马驹
foal

拖拉机
tractor

驴
donkey

羔羊
lamb

羊
sheep

山羊
goat

奶牛
cow

牛犊
calf

猪
pig

小猪
piglet

公牛
bull

鹅

goose

鸭

duck

小鸡

chick

母鸡

hen

公鸡

cockerel

鼠

rat

猫

cat

老鼠

mouse

牛

ox

狗

dog

狗屋

dog house

花园浇水软管

garden hose

洒水壶

watering can

长柄大镰刀

scythe

犁

plow

镰刀
sickle

锄头
hoe

长柄草耙
pitchfork

斧头
axe

独轮手推车
pushcart

饲料槽
trough

牛奶罐
milk can

麻布袋
sack

栅栏
fence

马厩
stable

温室
greenhouse

土壤
soil

种子
seed

肥料
fertilizer

联合收割机
combine harvester

收割

harvest

收割

harvest

山药

yams

小麦

wheat

大豆

soya

土豆

potato

玉米

corn

油菜籽

rapeseed

果树

fruit tree

树薯

manioc

谷物

grain

烟囱
chimney

屋顶
roof

落水管
downspout

窗户
window

车库
garage

门铃
doorbell

门
door

垃圾桶
trash can

信箱
mailbox

花园
garden

客厅
living room

浴室
bathroom

厨房
kitchen

卧室
bedroom

儿童房
kids room

餐厅
dining room

地板

floor

墙壁

wall

吊顶

ceiling

地窖

cellar

桑拿

sauna

阳台

balcony

露台

terrace

游泳池

pool

割草机

lawn mower

被单

sheet

床罩

bedspread

床

bed

扫帚

broom

水桶

bucket

开关

switch

壁纸
wallpaper

台灯
lamp

照片
picture

搁架
shelf

橱柜
cabinet

壁炉
fireplace

电视机
television

花
flower

垫子
cushion

沙发
sofa

花瓶
vase

遥控器
remote control

地毯

carpet

窗帘

drape

餐桌

table

椅子

chair

摇椅

rocking chair

扶手椅

armchair

书

book

毯子

blanket

装饰品

decoration

木柴

firewood

电影

film

高保真音响

stereo system

钥匙

key

报纸

newspaper

油画

painting

海报

poster

收音机

radio

笔记本

notebook

吸尘器

vacuum cleaner

仙人掌

cactus

蜡烛

candle

冰箱
fridge

微波炉
microwave oven

厨房秤
kitchen scales

洗洁精
laundry detergent

烤面包机
toaster

冰柜
freezer

烤箱
stove

垃圾桶
trash can

洗碗机
dishwasher

炊具

cooker

锅

pot

铸铁锅

cast-iron pot

炒锅

wok / kadai

平底锅

pan

水壶

kettle

蒸锅

steamer

烤盘

baking tray

陶瓷锅

crockery

马克杯

mug

碗

bowl

筷子

chopsticks

长柄勺

ladle

铲子

spatula

搅拌器

whisk

滤网

strainer

筛子

sieve

磨碎机

grater

研钵

mortar

烧烤

barbecue

明火

fireplace

菜板

chopping board

擀面杖

rolling pin

开瓶器

corkscrew

罐子

can

开罐器

can opener

隔热手套

oven cloth

水槽

sink

刷子

brush

海绵

sponge

搅拌机

blender

冷藏箱

deep freezer

奶瓶

baby bottle

水龙头

tap

供暖设备
heating

淋浴
shower

毛巾
towel

浴帘
shower curtain

泡沫浴
bubble bath

浴缸
bathtub

玻璃杯
glass

洗衣机
washing machine

瓷砖
tiles

水龙头
tap

便壶
potty

水槽
sink

厕所
toilet

蹲便器
squat toilet

坐浴器
bidet

小便池
urinal

厕纸
toilet paper

马桶刷
toilet brush

牙刷
toothbrush

牙膏
toothpaste

牙线
dental floss

洗
wash

手持式喷淋头
hand shower

冲洗器
douche

洗脸盆
basin

擦背刷
back brush

肥皂
soap

沐浴露
shower gel

洗发水
shampoo

法兰绒
flannel

排水
drain

乳霜
creme

除臭剂
deodorant

镜子

mirror

手镜

hand mirror

剃须刀

razor

剃须泡沫

shaving foam

须后水

aftershave

梳子

comb

刷子

brush

吹风机

hair-dryer

喷发定型剂

hairspray

化妆品

makeup

唇膏

lipstick

指甲油

nail varnish

化妆棉

cotton wool

指甲剪

nail scissors

香水

perfume

洗漱包

washbag

凳子

stool

计重秤

weighing scales

浴袍

bathrobe

橡胶手套

rubber gloves

卫生棉条

tampon

卫生巾

sanitary towel

化学厕所

chemical toilet

闹钟
alarm clock

毛绒玩具
cuddly toy

玩具车
toy car

拨浪鼓
rattle

玩具屋
doll's house

礼物
present

气球
balloon

床
bed

（洋娃娃用）婴儿车
stroller

扑克牌
deck of cards

拼图
jigsaw

漫画
comic

乐高积木

lego bricks

积木玩具

toy blocks

玩具人

action figure

婴儿服

romper suit

飞盘

frisbee

床铃玩具

mobile

棋盘游戏

board game

骰子

dice

火车模型

model train set

安抚奶嘴

pacifier

聚会

party

绘本

picture book

球

ball

洋娃娃

doll

玩

play

沙坑

sandpit

秋千

swing

玩具

toys

游戏机

video game console

三轮车

tricycle

泰迪熊

teddy bear

衣柜

wardrobe

衣服

clothing

袜子

socks

长袜

stockings

紧身裤

tights

围巾
scarf

皮带
belt

雨伞
umbrella

T恤
t-shirt

运动鞋
sneakers

靴子
boots

拖鞋
slippers

凉鞋

sandals

鞋

shoes

雨靴

rubber boots

内裤

underwear

胸罩

bra

背心

undershirt

衣服 - clothing

45

身体
body

裤子
pants

牛仔裤
jeans

短裙
skirt

女式衬衫
blouse

衬衫
shirt

套头衫
pullover

卫衣
sweater

西装夹克
blazer

夹克
jacket

外套
coat

雨衣
raincoat

套装
costume

连衣裙
dress

婚纱
wedding dress

西装

suit

睡袍

nightgown

睡衣

pajamas

莎丽

sari

头巾

headscarf

包头巾

turban

波卡

burka

卡夫坦

kaftan

(阿拉伯式)长袍长袍

abaya

泳衣

swimsuit

男式泳裤

trunks

短裤

shorts

运动服

tracksuit

围裙

apron

手套

gloves

纽扣
button

眼镜
glasses

手链
bracelet

项链
necklace

戒指
ring

耳环
earring

便帽
cap

衣架
coat hanger

帽子
hat

领带
tie

拉链
zip

头盔
helmet

背带
braces

校服
school uniform

制服
uniform

围兜
bib

安抚奶嘴
pacifier

尿不湿
diaper

服务器
server

文件柜
filing cabinet

打印机
printer

纸
paper

显示屏
monitor

鼠标
mouse

办公桌
desk

文件夹
folder

键盘
keyboard

废纸筐
waste-paper basket

椅子
chair

电脑
computer

咖啡杯
coffee mug

计算器
calculator

因特网
internet

笔记本电脑

laptop

信件

letter

消息

message

手机

cell phone

网络

network

复印机

photocopier

软件

software

电话

telephone

插座

plug socket

传真机

fax machine

表格

form

文件

document

买
buy

付钱
pay

交易
trade

现金
money

美元
dollar

欧元
euro

日元
yen

卢布
rouble

瑞士法郎
Swiss franc

人民币
renminbi yuan

卢比
rupee

提款处
cash point

外币兑换处

currency exchange office

金

gold

银

silver

石油

oil

能源

energy

价格

price

合同

contract

税金

tax

股票

stock

工作

work

职员

employee

老板

employer

工厂

factory

商店

shop

警官
police officer

消防员
fireman

厨师
cook

医生
doctor

飞行员
pilot

园丁

gardener

木匠

carpenter

裁缝

seamstress

法官

judge

化学家

chemist

演员

actor

公交车司机

bus driver

出租车司机

taxi driver

渔夫

fisherman

清洁女工

cleaning lady

屋顶工

roofer

服务员

waiter

猎人

hunter

画家

painter

面包师

baker

电工

electrician

建筑工人

builder

工程师

engineer

屠夫

butcher

水管工

plumber

邮递员

postman

士兵

soldier

建筑师

architect

收银员

cashier

花农

florist

理发师

hairdresser

售票员

conductor

机械师

mechanic

船长

captain

牙医

dentist

科学家

scientist

拉比

rabbi

伊玛目

imam

和尚

monk

牧师

pastor

铁锤
hammer

钳子
pliers

螺丝刀
screwdriver

扳手
wrench

手电筒
torch

挖掘机

excavator

工具箱

toolbox

梯子

ladder

锯子

saw

钉子

nails

钻机

drill

修
repair

铲子
shovel

靠！
Damn!

簸箕
dustpan

油漆桶
paint can

螺丝
screws

乐器
musical instruments

扬声器
loud speaker

打击乐器
drum set

吉他
guitar

▼低音提琴
double bass

小号
trumpet

钢琴

piano

小提琴

violin

贝斯

bass

定音鼓

timpani

鼓

drums

电子琴

keyboard

萨克斯管

saxophone

长笛

flute

麦克风

microphone

老虎
tiger

入口
entrance

笼子
cage

斑马
zebra

动物饲料
animal feed

熊猫
panda

动物

animals

大象

elephant

袋鼠

kangaroo

犀牛

rhino

大猩猩

gorilla

熊

bear

骆驼

camel

鸵鸟

ostrich

狮子

lion

猴子

monkey

火烈鸟

flamingo

鹦鹉

parrot

北极熊

polar bear

企鹅

penguin

鲨鱼

shark

孔雀

peacock

蛇

snake

鳄鱼

crocodile

动物园管理员

zookeeper

海豹

seal

美洲豹

jaguar

矮种马

pony

豹

leopard

河马

hippo

长颈鹿

giraffe

老鹰

eagle

野猪

boar

鱼

fish

龟

turtle

海象

walrus

狐狸

fox

羚羊

gazelle

橄榄球
American football

骑自行车
cycling

网球
tennis

篮球
basketball

游泳
swimming

拳击
boxing

冰球
ice hockey

英式足球
soccer

羽毛球
badminton

田径
athletics

手球
handball

滑雪
skiing

马球
polo

跳
jump

笑
laugh

拥抱
hug

走路
walk

唱
sing

祈祷
pray

亲吻
kiss

做梦
dream

书写
write

画
draw

展示
show

推
push

给
give

拿
take

有
have

做
do

当
be

站
stand

跑
run

拉
pull

扔
throw

摔倒
fall

躺
lie

等待
wait

携带
carry

坐
sit

穿衣
get dressed

睡觉
sleep

醒来
wake up

看
look at

哭
cry

抚摸
stroke

梳头
comb

交谈
talk

明白
understand

问
ask

听
listen

喝
drink

吃
eat

清理
tidy up

爱
love

做饭
cook

开车
drive

飞
fly

活动 - activities

航行

sail

计算

calculate

读

read

学习

learn

工作

work

结婚

marry

缝

sew

刷牙

brush teeth

杀

kill

抽烟

smoke

寄

send

祖母
grandmother

祖父
grandfather

父亲
father

母亲
mother

婴童
baby

女儿
daughter

儿子
son

客人

guest

阿姨

aunt

叔叔

uncle

兄弟

brother

姐妹

sister

前额
forehead

眼睛
eye

肩膀
shoulder

手指
finger

脸
face

下巴
chin

手
hand

乳房
breast

腿
leg

手臂
arm

婴童
baby

男人
man

女人
woman

女孩
girl

男孩
boy

头
head

背部
back

肚子
belly

肚脐
navel

脚趾
toe

脚后跟
heel

骨头
bone

臀部
hip

膝盖
knee

手肘
elbow

鼻子
nose

屁股
buttocks

皮肤
skin

脸颊
cheek

耳朵
ear

嘴唇
lip

身体 - body

嘴

mouth

牙齿

tooth

舌头

tongue

脑

brain

心脏

heart

肌肉

muscle

肺

lung

肝脏

liver

胃

stomach

肾脏

kidneys

性交

sex

避孕套

condom

卵子

ovum

精子

semen

怀孕

pregnancy

月经

menstruation

阴道

vagina

阴茎

penis

眉毛

eyebrow

头发

hair

脖子

neck

身体 - body

医院
hospital

救护车
ambulance

轮椅
wheelchair

骨折
fracture

医生

doctor

急诊室

emergency room

护士

nurse

紧急情况

emergency

昏迷

unconscious

痛

pain

受伤

injury

出血

bleeding

心脏病发作

heart attack

中风

stroke

过敏

allergy

咳嗽

cough

发烧

fever

流感

flu

腹泻

diarrhea

头痛

headache

癌症

cancer

糖尿病

diabetes

外科医生

surgeon

手术刀

scalpel

手术

operation

CT

CT

X光

x-ray

超声波

ultrasound

口罩

face mask

疾病

disease

候诊室

waiting room

拐杖

crutch

石膏

plaster

绷带

bandage

注射

injection

听诊器

stethoscope

担架

stretcher

体温计

clinical thermometer

出生

birth

超重

overweight

助听器

hearing aid

消毒液

disinfectant

感染

infection

病毒

virus

艾滋病

HIV / AIDS

药物

medicine

接种疫苗

vaccination

药片

tablets

药丸

pill

急救电话

emergency call

血压计

blood pressure monitor

生病/健康

ill / healthy

医院 - hospital

救命！
Help!

警报
alarm

突击
assault

攻击
attack

危险
danger

紧急出口
emergency exit

着火啦！
Fire!

灭火器
fire extinguisher

意外
accident

急救箱
first-aid kit

呼救信号
SOS

警察
police

欧洲

Europe

北美洲

North America

南美洲

South America

非洲

Africa

亚洲

Asia

澳洲

Australia

大西洋

Atlantic

太平洋

Pacific

印度洋

Indian Ocean

南冰洋

Antarctic Ocean

北冰洋

Arctic Ocean

北极

North pole

南极

South pole

南极洲

Antarctica

地球

earth

陆地

land

海

sea

岛

island

国家

nation

国家

state

地球 - earth

钟面

clock face

时针

hour hand

分针

minute hand

秒针

second hand

现在几点？

What time is it?

天

day

时间

time

现在

now

电子表

digital watch

分

minute

时

hour

周一 Monday

周三 Wednesday

周五 Friday

MO

W

FR

TU

TH

SA

SO

周二 Tuesday

周六 Saturday

周四 Thursday

周日 Sunday

昨天

yesterday

今天

today

明天

tomorrow

早晨

morning

中午

noon

晚上

evening

工作日

workdays

周末

weekend

雨
rain

彩虹
rainbow

雪
snow

风
wind

春
spring

秋
fall

夏
summer

冬
winter

天气预报
weather forecast

温度计
thermometer

阳光
sunshine

云
cloud

雾
fog

潮湿
humidity

闪电

lightning

打雷

thunder

风暴

storm

冰雹

hail

季风

monsoon

洪水

flood

冰

ice

一月

January

二月

February

三月

March

四月

April

五月

May

六月

June

七月

July

八月

August

九月

September

十月

October

十一月

November

十二月

December

形状

shapes

圆形

circle

正方形

square

长方形

rectangle

三角形

triangle

球体

sphere

立方体

cube

白

white

黄

yellow

橙

orange

粉

pink

红

red

紫

purple

蓝

blue

绿

green

棕

brown

灰

gray

黑

black

很多/少许

a lot / a little

生气/平静

angry / calm

美/丑

beautiful / ugly

首/尾

beginning / end

大/小

big / small

明/暗

bright / dark

兄弟/姐妹

brother / sister

干净/肮脏

clean / dirty

完整/缺失

complete / incomplete

白天/晚上

day / night

死/生

dead / alive

宽/窄

wide / narrow

可食用/非食用

edible / inedible

邪恶/善良

evil / kind

兴奋/无聊

excited / bored

胖/瘦

fat / thin

第一/最后

first / last

朋友/敌人

friend / enemy

满/空

full / empty

硬/软

hard / soft

重/轻

heavy / light

饿/渴

hunger / thirst

生病/健康

ill / healthy

非法/合法

illegal / legal

聪明/愚笨

intelligent / stupid

左/右

left / right

近/远

near / far

新/旧

new / used

没有/有些

nothing / something

老/幼

old / young

开/关

on / off

打开/合上

open / closed

安静/吵闹

quiet / loud

富/穷

rich / poor

对/错

right / wrong

粗糙/光滑

rough / smooth

伤心/高兴

sad / happy

短/长

short / long

慢/快

slow / fast

湿/干

wet / dry

温暖/凉爽

warm / cool

战争/和平

war / peace

反义词 - opposites

0

零
....
zero

1

一
....
one

2

二
....
two

3

三
....
three

4

四
....
four

5

五
....
five

6

六
....
six

7

七
....
seven

8

八
....
eight

9

九
....
nine

10

十
....
ten

11

十一
....
eleven

12

十二

twelve

13

十三

thirteen

14

十四

fourteen

15

十五

fifteen

16

十六

sixteen

17

十七

seventeen

18

十八

eighteen

19

十九

nineteen

20

二十

twenty

100

百

hundred

1.000

千

thousand

1.000.000

百万

million

语言
languages

英语
English

美式英语
American English

普通话
Chinese Mandarin

印地语
Hindi

西班牙语
Spanish

法语
French

阿拉伯语
Arabic

俄语
Russian

葡萄牙语
Portuguese

孟加拉语
Bengali

德语
German

日语
Japanese

我

I

你

you

他/她/它

he / she / it

我们

we

你们

you

他们

they

谁？

who?

什么？

what?

怎样？

how?

哪里？

where?

什么时候？

when?

名字

name

方位

where

后面

behind

里面

in

前面

in front of

上方

over

上面

on

下面

under

旁边

beside

中间

between

地点

place